I0753722

FINISHING LINE PRESS
www.finishinglinepress.com

Haiku for the Journey

Poems by

Cynthia T. Hahn

Illustrations by

Monique Loubet

Finishing Line Press
Georgetown, Kentucky

Haiku for the Journey

ISBN 979-8-89990-390-8 First Edition

ACKNOWLEDGMENTS

Modified versions of poems "Aftermath" and "Intermission" (II) were published in *Collage Magazine* (Lake Forest College, 2022-23), pp. 52-60. A modified, untitled version of "Winter Breaks and Falls" appeared in *Whispers of the Seasons: A Contemporary Haiku Anthology.* Editor Som. (Fresh Words-An International Literary Magazine, 2025), p. 6. Images 1, 2, 7, 9 appeared in excerpted or altered format in the poet and artist's first collaborative volume, *Co-ïncidences* (Paris: alfAbarre, 2014).

Publisher: Leah Huete de Maines
Editor: Christen Kincaid
Cover Art and Artist Photo: Monique Loubet.
Author Photo: Richard Nowson
Cover Design: Elizabeth Maines McCleavy

Order online: www.finishinglinepress.com
also available on amazon.com

Author inquiries and mail orders:
Finishing Line Press
PO Box 1626
Georgetown, Kentucky 40324
USA

Contents

This text is dedicated to writer-artist friends who inspire me, especially Monique, Evelyne, Kathy, Lois, Karin, Verena, to garden-co-creator Richard, and to my father, aspiring poet. —Cynthia T. Hahn, author

*

Je dédie ce livre à mon compagnon Jean-Pierre La Porte, à notre parcours ensemble, poète dans l'âme, lecteur assidu si sensible à mes oeuvres. —Monique Loubet, artist

I spied a haiku
blooming in the woods today;
it followed me home.

***

These haikus, written in a classic syllabic 5/7/5 form, are intended to capture the wonder of sensory moments gathered from garden, forest and ocean walks; they span seasonal time and encourage meditation upon connections we make to the natural world, of which humans comprise but a very small part.

The illustrations were chosen to add color and texture to the poetic dimension, prompting the reader to linger and deepen the space for reflective pause.

I. Autumnal quickening

Tending to Storm

I.

Wind nearing silence.
These dark days, pulling rabbits
from black cloud top hats.

II.

Mad rain, pulling its
clouded grief to still darker
hills, drowns itself there.

III.

Wet clouds tremble and
swell, strewing low the snow shells,
while a stone path shrinks.

Aftermath

I.

My steps chase the slick
rain from mirrored stones, storm
shimmers found and lost.

II.

Cardinal passes,
her shadow descends to cool
bricks, the waning red.

III.

Black and grey wing has
lost a feather to these stones;
small thunder passing.

Intermission

I.

Geese trailing their notes:
suspended sky coda and
overture calling

II.

Wise pine bends the wind
plying borrowed branch; rooted trunk
beats solid and deep.

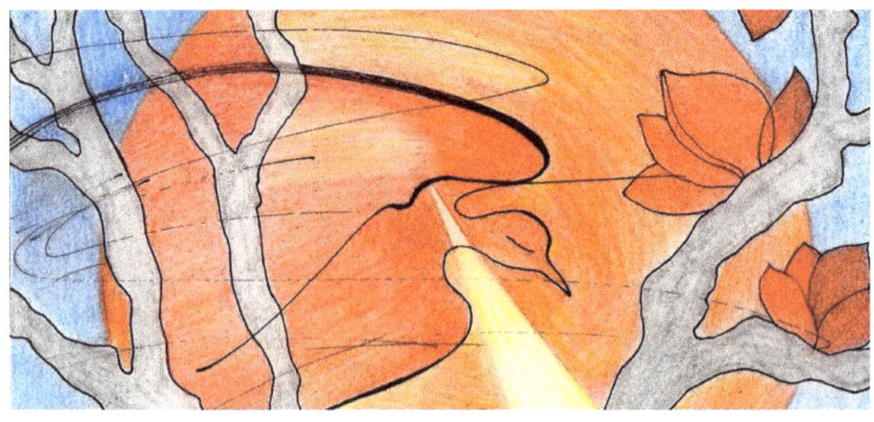

Tail End

I.

The long yawn falls in
late October, sustaining
hibernation gold.

II.

November sun sets
and slumbers, low crimson dark
ashen cloud embers.

III.

Ginger cat kneads wool
grey shawl, whiskers touching sleep;
tail flicks a night watch.

II. Lightening Up

Early Drift

I.

Tracked path, the snowy
half moons filling shadow shells
with drops of spring sun.

II.

Wind encircles wide
plum-budding branches, they sway
a seasonal rift.

III.

Breeze sailing deftly
with sparrows under fronds of
Alaskan Cypress.

Winter Breaks and Falls

Full snow fiesta
morning blooms in bright, white gold.
Origami stars.

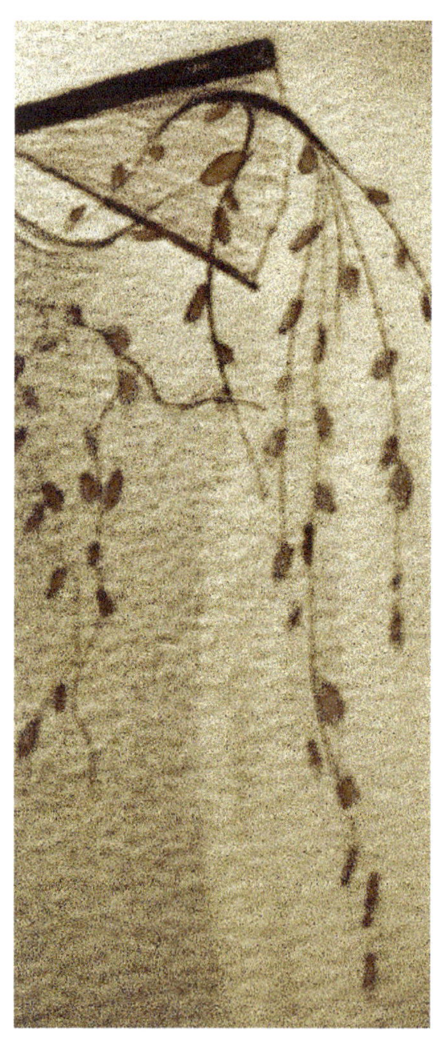

Spring Stir

I.

Pearly pear aloft;
snowfall-setting petals preen,
staging swaths of green.

II.

Tan branch spurs wings of
unfurling leaf; silken green
pages now turning.

III.

We brush against the
harpstring maple; her branches
at play, soft dulcet.

Mizzle

Breathing in this rain,
open-mouthed, my tongue reborn,
soft green whispering.

Traces

I.

Spring snake crosses our
boots on its path; stopped glances
charmed by a shimmer.

II.

Bullfrog sounds drum song ...
our djembes echo the thrum,
solos beat as one.

III.

Streak of lightning strikes
silvered cool, lake's swirling wake:
moon shivers anew.

III. Threading Summer Song

Morning Brights

I.

Dew on the gingko,
butterfly diamonds glisten;
on the plum, rubies.

II.

June Canna lily,
miracle of pink fingers;
light turning to swoon.

III.

We are all flowers.
How we forget—still we bend
whenever we bloom.

Light portraits

I.

Moss forest at dawn;
light shimmies your tall-stemmed trunks,
magnifies the earth.

II.

Dark-leafed full forest,
top branch stretches dreams of flight;
bird splay, hovering.

III.

Cleaving the pewter,
misted cloud breaks into rings ...
my oar, a paintbrush.

Dusk Aria

—For Karin

I.

Light behind stratus
sets the stage for singular
rose curtain sky play.

II.

Fledgling within a
cascade of elder cherry,
trills the evening home.

III.

Broad waves of fireworks
eclipse the stars, our eyes small
mirrors to the sky.

Evening respite

I.

Sapphire night dives; a
moonsong silver spills a new
path, pale teahouse guest.

II.

Summer thrum, brushing
cicada strands of night wind,
lifting purple plum.

III.

Lanterns sighting this
garden stroll, calling fireflies,
scattering small moons.

IV. Ocean Time

Tidal Pull

Rolling in spring’s berth,
gentle surf curls round my step,
sea bird sky alight.

Cape Perpetua

I.

Resonant shell's ear
brims Pacific roil and pull,
awash on whale rock.

II.

Straddling somber greys,
porous eye of tide rises—
thunderous cloud spray.

Cape Perpetua (bis)

I.

Orange stars, small suns
suspended in pool shimmer,
wind spur caressing.

II.

Soft-spoken velvet
moss curtain free falls down tall
spires of Sitka Spruce.

III.

Creek spills its secret,
carries it freshly spoken,
running to ocean.

Beach Grove

Sky cracks, scarlet streaks.
I shelter with low, blue pine.
One sigh sets the sun.

Author:

Cynthia T. Hahn has authored two volumes of poetry, *Outside-In-Sideout* (Finishing Line Press, 2010), a text on the emotional landscape of grief, and *Co-ïncidences,* bilingual self-translated, with illustrations by Parisian artist Monique Loubet (alfAbarre Press, Paris, 2014), poetic and visual portraits of moments along life's path. A Professor of French at Lake Forest College, IL, teaching creative writing and translation since 1990, Cynthia Hahn is a member of two writer's groups, Highland Park Poets and Bluff Coast Writers. Hahn has translated over ten novels by Algerian, French and Lebanese authors. Over 100 of her poems have appeared in journals such as *The Ekphrastic Review, East on Central, Last Stanza Journal, Highland Park Poets,* online chosen as "Best of the Net", and in a number of anthologies such as *The Memory Palace.* Her personal sanctuary and locus of inspiration for her writing is her Japanese-style garden.

Artist:

Monique Loubet resided in the American Midwest during the 1960s, where she studied acrylic painting at Anderson College (Indiana). Returning to France in the early 1970s, Loubet studied lithography and linocut printmaking for two years at the École des Beaux-Arts in Paris, then began to include India ink and pastels in her creative work. In 1979, her tableaux featured in the Salon d'automne at the Grand Palais, and she joined the "Groupe des peintres du Marais," exhibiting in many solo and group shows. More recently, she has illustrated several literary works, including the cover and art for this second collaborative volume with Cynthia Hahn.

www.ingramcontent.com/pod-product-compliance
Lightning Source LLC
LaVergne TN
LVHW052357100826
845147LV00013B/868

* 9 7 9 8 8 9 9 9 0 3 9 0 8 *